great grilling

great grilling

louise pickford

photography by Ian Wallace

RYLAND
PETERS
& SMALL

LONDON NEW YORK

Senior Designer   Paul Tilby
Commissioning Editor   Elsa Petersen-Schepelern
Editor   Sharon Cochrane
Production   Paul Harding
Editorial Director   Julia Charles
Art Director   Anne-Marie Bulat
Publishing Director   Alison Starling

First published in the USA in 2006
by Ryland Peters & Small, Inc.
519 Broadway, 5th Floor
New York, NY 10012
www.rylandpeters.com

10 9 8 7 6 5 4 3 2 1

Library of Congress Cataloging-in-Publication Data

Pickford, Louise.
    Great grilling / Louise Pickford ; photography
by Ian Wallace.
       p. cm.
    Includes index.
    ISBN-13: 978-1-84597-203-5
    ISBN-10: 1-84597-203-1
    1. Barbecue cookery. I. Title.
    TX840.B3P499 2006
    641.5'784--dc22
                                        2005028006

Printed in China

NOTE

Uncooked eggs should not be served to the very young, the very old, those with compromised immune systems, or to pregnant women.

All photography by Ian Wallace except page 76 by Peter Cassidy.

contents

introduction

Today we associate grilling and barbecuing with being outdoors, and therefore countries with warmer climates tend to be better equipped for this type of cooking. Now I am based in Australia, it has become very attractive indeed. The result is this book–a celebration of my passion and enthusiasm for this age-old method of outdoor cooking on the grill.

The word "barbecue" is derived from the Spanish word *barbacoa* and has several meanings: one is to cook over dry heat, such as coals; another is the equipment on which this is done; and a third is the meal itself–sometimes something as large as a party. It seems to have originated in the Caribbean and Florida, then migrated across the South, where barbecuing became a way of life. Barbecues as social gatherings can be traced back to when plantation owners held massive barbecues for friends, families, and townspeople.

Which is best–charcoal or gas? Having tested these recipes using both types, I can offer an opinion. For flavor I would choose a charcoal grill, but for convenience the gas version wins hands down, especially if you are cooking for two. Imagine heating the coals for up to 40 minutes, then searing a tuna steak for one minute on each side. Of course, you can buy small charcoal grills where you need only heat up a few coals, but turning a dial and pressing the ignite button on a gas grill is far more efficient and appealing. The same argument might apply to electric grills, but I think these are a bit like regular stoves. Yes–for a barbecue, we need real fire!

When the weather isn't good enough for lighting the grill, or when there are only a few people to cook for and you want to do so quickly, a stovetop grill pan is the perfect alternative. Most of the recipes in this book can be cooked on a grill pan, giving you all the flavor of a grill without the smoke and fuss. So even if the sun isn't shining, you can enjoy the delights of grilled food all year round.

WHICH GRILL?

There are three main categories of grill to choose from—charcoal/wood, gas, or electric.

Charcoal grills, mostly designed to burn both coals and wood, are messy to use, take a long time to prepare, and need constant attention, but the food has that distinctive smoky caramelized flavor we love so much. The exterior of the food is sticky and char-grilled while the interior remains moist and succulent.

A gas grill on the other hand can be lit in seconds and the temperature set with the twist of a dial. It is easy to clean with no hot coals to worry about at the end. Most gas grills have a flat plate as well as a regular grill so you can cook every cut of meat or type of fish with ease. If you're cooking for just one or two people, they can save you time and money. The end result will taste good but may not have that char-grilled flavor of charcoal or wood.

Food cooked on an electric grill will also lack that special smoky flavor, but this style of grill does have the advantage of being usable where one with an open flame would not be suitable—in high-rise buildings, for example, or on total-fire-ban days.

A stovetop grill pan will give you a smoky flavor but none of the thrills of cooking outdoors or for a large group of people.

Weighing up the choices, it seems that the ideal solution is to have several kinds on hand. This is for two reasons; first, if you are cooking for just one or two people gas is probably a more sensible option—or, for a larger crowd, then I prefer to cook over coals when it's worth all the extra effort.

CHOOSING A CHARCOAL GRILL

The disposable grill sets available from many supermarkets or hardware stores are ideal for the "once-in-a-while" backyard barbecue.

The highly portable grills, such as the cast-iron Hibachi from Japan (available worldwide), are small and relatively inexpensive. They are usually vented to help to increase or decrease the heat or have a rung system above the coals so the grill rack can be low or high as necessary.

The table grill is really a box on legs. The box, called a grate, takes the coals, with the grill rack for cooking above that. Again the rack can be raised or lowered as necessary. Make sure that the legs are sturdy before buying this type of grill.

Kettle grills, such as Weber, are very versatile. The kettle-shaped drum protects the fire from wind or rain and the dome-shaped lid transforms it into an oven. The vent system on a kettle grill also makes it easier to control the temperature—wide-open vents creating a hotter fire, while closed vents will extinguish it.

CHOOSING A GAS GRILL

Gas grills are available in all shapes, sizes, and prices—you just have to decide how often you're going to use it, how many people you will be cooking for, and exactly what you want your grill to do.

The cheapest is the simple gas grill, shaped like a table with gas burners rather than charcoal. It usually has both a flat plate and a grill section.

Middle range gas grills will have a lid and often have side attachments, including shelves. The gas grill on

wheels has a dome-shaped lid and may include side attachments such as shelves for stacking plates, or an extra round burner designed to hold a wok. It may have a thermometer device and a rotisserie attachment.

Top-end super-grills include "everything but the kitchen sink" for the true grilling enthusiast. Often made in stainless steel, they are quite magnificent and will include all the bells and whistles listed above, plus a separate smoker box.

CHOOSING AN ELECTRIC GRILL

There are several varieties of electric grill on the market and although they may lack the flame-grill flavor of gas, charcoal, or wood, they still have appeal. When you are buying an electric grill always check that the legs are sturdy and that the grill has a thermostat. The special advantages of an electric grill are:

• Ideal for a deck area where sparks could be dangerous and are particularly suited to high-rise living.

• Easily regulated with a thermostat for accurate and instant temperature control.

• Great for impromptu cooking.

• Some can be used for smoking.

CHOOSING A STOVETOP GRILL PAN

Grill pans come in many shapes and sizes. Buy the biggest pan you can find, then you will be able to cook a few grilled vegetables at the same time as meat, poultry or fish. Cast-iron pans are heavy and sturdy and may need seasoning before use, while aluminum versions are lighter and often have a nonstick surface.

vegetables

Serving a large platter of grilled vegetables provides a lovely start to any barbecue party—choose a combination of your favorites. A delicious way to serve them is on a bed of grilled polenta or accompanied by some fresh, crusty bread.

vegetable **antipasto**

2 red bell peppers

4 baby fennel bulbs

1 large eggplant

1 red onion

2 large zucchini

1 recipe Herb, Lemon, and Garlic Marinade (page 94)

a few fresh herb leaves, such as basil, dill, fennel, mint, and parsley

extra virgin olive oil, to taste

freshly squeezed lemon juice, to taste

sea salt and freshly ground black pepper

crusty bread or grilled polenta, to serve

SERVES 4

Cut the peppers into quarters and remove and discard the seeds. Trim the fennel, reserving the fronds, and cut the bulbs into ¼-inch slices. Cut the eggplant into thick slices and cut in half again. Cut the onion into wedges and cut the zucchini into thick slices diagonally.

Put all the vegetables in a large bowl, pour over the marinade, and toss gently until evenly coated. Cover and let marinate in a cool place for at least 1 hour.

Preheat the grill or stovetop grill pan, add the vegetables, and cook until they are all tender and lightly charred. Let cool, then peel the peppers.

Arrange the vegetables on a large platter, sprinkle with the herbs, reserved fennel fronds, olive oil, and lemon juice, then season lightly with salt and pepper. Serve at room temperature with crusty bread or grilled polenta.

11

grilled artichokes with chile-lime mayonnaise

Try to find small or baby artichokes for this dish so that they can be cooked straight on the grill without any blanching first.

18 small artichokes

1 lemon, cut in half

2 tablespoons extra virgin olive oil

sea salt and freshly ground black pepper

lime wedges, to serve

CHILE-LIME MAYONNAISE

1 dried chipotle chile

2 egg yolks

1¼ cups olive oil

freshly squeezed juice of 1 lime

SERVES 6

To make the mayonnaise, cover the chipotle with boiling water and let soak for 30 minutes. Drain and pat dry, then cut in half and scrape out the seeds.

Finely chop the chile flesh and put in a food processor. Add the egg yolks and a little salt and blend briefly until frothy. With the blade running, gradually pour the oil through the funnel until the sauce is thick and glossy. Add the lime juice and, if the mayonnaise is too thick, 1 tablespoon warm water. Taste and adjust the seasoning with salt and pepper, if necessary, then cover and set aside.

Trim the stalks from the artichokes and cut off the top 1 inch of the globes. Slice the globes in half lengthwise, cutting out the central "choke" if necessary. Rub the cut surfaces with lemon juice to stop them discoloring.

Toss the artichokes with the oil and a little salt and pepper. Cook over medium-hot coals or on a preheated stovetop grill pan for 15 to 20 minutes, depending on size, until charred and tender, turning halfway through the cooking time. Serve with the mayonnaise and wedges of lime.

Vegetables taste wonderful when cooked on the grill—it brings out their natural sweetness. This salad will serve four as an entrée or six as an appetizer.

roasted red bell pepper and asparagus salad

Put the onion slices in a strainer, sprinkle with salt, and let drain over a bowl for 30 minutes. Rinse the onion under cold running water and pat dry with paper towels.

Preheat the grill, then cook the peppers over hot coals for 15 minutes, turning frequently until charred all over. Alternatively, cook the peppers on a preheated stovetop grill pan. Transfer to a plastic bag, seal, and let soften until cool. Peel off the skin and discard the seeds, then cut the flesh into thick strips.

Brush the asparagus with olive oil and cook over hot coals or on the stovetop grill pan for 3 to 4 minutes, turning frequently, until charred and tender.

Put the snowpeas in a large saucepan of lightly salted boiling water and cook for 1 to 2 minutes. Drain and refresh under cold running water.

Put the onion, peppers, asparagus, and snowpeas in a large bowl and toss gently. Add the salad leaves, herbs, and hazelnuts. Put all the dressing ingredients in a bowl and beat well. Season to taste with salt and pepper, then pour over the salad and toss well to coat. Serve immediately.

½ red onion, sliced

6 red bell peppers

1 lb. asparagus, trimmed

extra virgin olive oil, for brushing

8 oz. snowpeas

4 oz. mixed salad leaves

a handful of fresh parsley and dill

2 oz. hazelnuts, about ¾ cup, toasted and coarsely chopped

HAZELNUT OIL DRESSING

¼ cup hazelnut oil

2 tablespoons extra virgin olive oil

1 tablespoon sherry vinegar

1 teaspoon sugar

sea salt and freshly ground black pepper

SERVES 4–6

The nut sauce, tarator, served with these leeks is found in Middle Eastern cooking, though cooks there would use ground almonds or walnuts. If you make the sauce in advance, beat it well before use.

charred leeks with tarator sauce

1½ lb. baby leeks, trimmed

2–3 tablespoons extra virgin olive oil

a few lemon wedges, to serve

TARATOR SAUCE

2 oz. macadamia nuts, toasted

1 oz. fresh bread crumbs, ½ cup

2 garlic cloves, crushed

½ cup extra virgin olive oil

1 tablespoon freshly squeezed lemon juice

sea salt and freshly ground black pepper

SERVES 4

To make the sauce, put the nuts in a food processor and grind coarsely, then add the bread crumbs, garlic, and salt and pepper and process again to form a smooth paste. Transfer to a bowl and very gradually beat in the olive oil, lemon juice, and 2 tablespoons boiling water to form a sauce. Season to taste with salt and pepper.

Preheat the grill. Brush the leeks with a little olive oil, season with salt, and cook over medium-hot coals for 6 to 10 minutes, turning occasionally until charred and tender. Alternatively, cook the leeks on a preheated stovetop grill pan. Transfer to a plate, sprinkle with olive oil, pour the sauce over the top, and serve with the lemon wedges.

grilled corn with chile-salt rub

One of the Southwest's most popular chiles is the ancho, the dried version of the poblano. When ground to a fine powder, it has a smoky flavor and is mild to medium on the heat scale—delicious with the sweet, nutty taste of corn.

6 ears of corn, husks removed

2 tablespoons extra virgin olive oil, plus extra to serve

3 ancho chiles

1½ tablespoons sea salt, plus extra for cooking the corn

3 limes, cut into wedges

SERVES 6

Trim the ends of the corn. Bring a large saucepan of lightly salted water to a boil, add the corn, and boil for 1 to 2 minutes. Drain and refresh under cold water. Pat dry with paper towels.

Preheat an outdoor grill or stovetop grill pan until hot. Brush the corn with oil and cook for 5 to 7 minutes, turning frequently until charred all over.

Meanwhile, remove the stalk and seeds from the ancho chiles. Chop the flesh coarsely and, using a spice grinder or mortar and pestle, grind to a powder. Transfer to a small bowl, then mix in the salt.

Rub the lime wedges vigorously over the corn, sprinkle with the chile salt, and serve with extra oil for drizzling.

Just the ticket for people who don't eat meat but love a good burger. The onion jam can be made ahead and kept in the refrigerator for several days.

mushroom burgers
with chile mayonnaise and onion jam

1 fresh hot red chile, about 2 inches long, seeded and chopped

about ½ cup mayonnaise

2 tablespoons extra virgin olive oil

4 large portobello mushrooms, stems trimmed

4 hamburger buns, split in half

salad leaves

sea salt and freshly ground black pepper

ONION JAM

2 tablespoons olive oil

2 red onions, thinly sliced

¼ cup red currant jelly

1 tablespoon red wine vinegar

SERVES 4

To make the onion jam, heat the olive oil in a saucepan, add the onions, and sauté gently for 15 minutes or until very soft. Add a pinch of salt, the red currant jelly, vinegar, and 2 tablespoons water and cook for another 15 minutes or until the mixture is glossy with a jam-like consistency. Remove from the heat and let cool.

Preheat the grill, then cook the chile whole over hot coals for 1 to 2 minutes or until the skin is charred and blackened. Alternatively, cook on a preheated stovetop grill pan. Transfer to a plastic bag, seal, and let cool slightly. Peel the chile, then remove and discard the seeds. Chop the flesh and transfer to a food processor. Add the mayonnaise and process until the sauce is speckled red. Taste and adjust the seasoning with salt and pepper, if necessary.

Brush the olive oil over the mushrooms, season well with salt and pepper, and cook on the grill rack or pan, stem side down, for 5 minutes. Using a spatula, flip the mushrooms and cook them on the other side for about 5 minutes until they are tender.

Toast the split buns for a few minutes on the grill or pan, then fill them with the mushrooms, salad leaves, onion jam, and a spoonful of the chile mayonnaise.

Orzo is a rice-shaped pasta, ideal for making into a salad because it retains its shape and texture very well when cooked.

orzo salad with lemon and herb dressing

Preheat the grill or broiler. Thread the tomatoes onto the soaked wooden skewers with all the cut halves facing the same way. Sprinkle with a little olive oil, season with salt and pepper, and grill or broil for 1 to 2 minutes on each side until lightly charred and softened. Remove from the heat and set aside while you cook the orzo.

Bring a large saucepan of lightly salted water to a boil. Add the orzo and cook for about 9 minutes or until "al dente." Drain well and transfer to a large bowl.

Heat 2 tablespoons olive oil in a skillet, add the herbs, scallions, and lemon zest, and stir-fry for 30 seconds. Stir into the orzo, then add the grilled tomatoes, lemon juice, the remaining olive oil, and salt and pepper. Toss well and let cool before serving.

Note Orzo is available at most large supermarkets. If you can't find it, use other small pasta shapes, such as ditalini or pennetti instead.

8 oz. cherry tomatoes, cut in half

⅓ cup extra virgin olive oil

8 oz. orzo or other tiny soup pasta*

¼ cup coarsely chopped mixed fresh herbs, such as basil, dill, mint, and parsley

6 scallions, finely chopped

grated zest and juice of 2 unwaxed lemons

sea salt and freshly ground black pepper

4 wooden skewers, soaked in water for 30 minutes

SERVES 4

This refreshing summer salad with a bright note of fresh mint makes a superb accompaniment to barbecued meat or fish.

zucchini, feta, and mint salad

1 tablespoon sesame seeds

6 medium zucchini

3 tablespoons extra virgin olive oil

6 oz. feta cheese, crumbled

a handful of fresh mint leaves

sea salt and freshly ground black pepper

DRESSING

¼ cup extra virgin olive oil

1 tablespoon freshly squeezed lemon juice

1 small garlic clove, crushed

SERVES 4

Toast the sesame seeds in a dry skillet over medium heat until golden and aromatic. Remove from the pan, let cool, and set aside until required.

Preheat the grill or stovetop grill pan. Cut the zucchini diagonally into thick slices, toss with the olive oil, and season with salt and pepper. Cook over hot coals or on the pan for 2 to 3 minutes on each side until charred and tender. Remove and let cool.

Put all the dressing ingredients in a screw-top jar and shake well. Season to taste with salt and pepper.

Put the zucchini, feta, and mint in a large bowl, add the dressing, and toss well until evenly coated. Sprinkle with the sesame seeds and serve at once.

8 oz. fresh mozzarella
cheese, drained

1 large green bell pepper,
seeded and diced

1 small cucumber, diced

2 ripe tomatoes, chopped

½ red onion,
finely chopped

2 pita breads

⅓–¼ cup extra virgin
olive oil

freshly squeezed juice
of ½ lemon

sea salt and freshly ground
black pepper

OLIVE SALSA

3 oz. Kalamata olives,
pitted and chopped

1 tablespoon chopped
fresh flat-leaf parsley

1 small garlic clove,
finely chopped

¼ cup extra virgin olive oil

1 tablespoon freshly
squeezed lemon juice

SERVES 4

Fatoush is a bread salad made from grilled pita bread. It's often accompanied by haloumi, a firm cheese that can be char-grilled. Fresh mozzarella cheese can also be cooked on the grill. It picks up an appealing smokiness in the process.

grilled pita salad
with olive salsa and mozzarella

Preheat the grill or stovetop grill pan. Wrap the mozzarella in paper towels and squeeze to remove excess water. Unwrap and cut into thick slices. Brush the slices well with olive oil. Cook over hot coals or on the pan for 1 minute on each side until the cheese is charred with lines and beginning to soften. Alternatively, simply slice the cheese and use without grilling.

Put the green pepper, cucumber, tomatoes, and onion in a bowl. Toast the pita breads over hot coals or on the stovetop grill pan. Let cool slightly, then tear into bite-size pieces. Add to the bowl, then pour over 1 to 2 tablespoons olive oil and a little lemon juice. Season with salt and pepper and stir well.

Put all the ingredients for the salsa in a bowl and stir well.

Spoon the salad onto appetizer plates, top with a few slices of mozzarella and some olive salsa, and serve.

beet hummus with pan-grilled bread

Beet hummus is a delicious summery dip for vegetables or toasted bread. Cooking bread on the grill or a stovetop grill pan is easy and very like the traditional way that pita bread is cooked.

8 oz. cooked beets in natural juices, drained and chopped

½ cup white bread crumbs

1 garlic clove, crushed

3 tablespoons extra virgin olive oil

2 tablespoons grated horseradish

1 tablespoon freshly squeezed lemon juice

sea salt and freshly ground black pepper

BREAD

2¼ cups bread flour, plus extra for kneading

1 teaspoon sea salt

1 teaspoon active dry yeast

1 tablespoon olive oil, plus extra for oiling

SERVES 6

To make the bread dough, sift the flour into the bowl of an electric mixer* with the dough hook attached. Stir in the salt and yeast, then gradually work in ⅓ cup warm water and the oil to make a soft dough. Transfer to a lightly floured surface and knead for 8 to 10 minutes until smooth and elastic.

Put the dough in an oiled bowl, cover with plastic wrap, and let rise in a warm place for 45 minutes or until doubled in size.

Meanwhile, to make the hummus, put the beets, bread crumbs, garlic, oil, horseradish, and lemon juice in a food processor, blend to a smooth purée, and season to taste with salt and pepper.

Transfer the dough to a lightly floured surface and knead gently. Divide it into 6 even pieces and roll out each one to an oval, about the size of a pita bread. Cook the bread on an oiled grill rack over medium-hot coals or on a preheated stovetop grill pan for 1 to 2 minutes on each side. Serve warm with the beet hummus.

*__*Note__ If you don't have an electric mixer, make the bread dough using a food processor with the plastic blade attachment, or make it by hand in a large bowl. Gradually work the mixture together with your hands to form a soft dough, then invert onto a lightly floured surface and knead for 8 to 10 minutes until the dough becomes smooth and elastic. Continue as in the main recipe, above.

Gooey, caramelized garlic spread over lightly char-grilled toast is the perfect appetizer to amuse your guests while you cook the entrée. It tastes absolutely amazing!

bruschetta with caramelized garlic

1 whole head of garlic

a sprig of fresh thyme

1 tablespoon extra virgin olive oil, plus extra for drizzling

4 slices of sourdough or ciabatta bread

sea salt and freshly ground black pepper

SERVES 4

Cut the top off the garlic head to reveal the cloves. Set the head on a piece of foil, add the thyme sprig, and season with salt and pepper. Sprinkle with the olive oil, then fold over the foil, sealing the edges to form a package.

Preheat the grill, then cook the garlic package over hot coals for 20 minutes or until the garlic is softened. Alternatively, cook the garlic in the foil package in a preheated oven at 400°F for about 40 minutes until the garlic is tender.

Put the bread slices on the grill rack and toast for a few minutes on each side. Squeeze the cooked garlic out of the cloves and spread onto the toasted bread. Sprinkle with a little more olive oil, season with salt and pepper, and serve warm.

VARIATION Try topping the garlic with slices of Camembert cheese and sprinkling with extra virgin olive oil.

This is a fun version of garlic bread, and the slightly smoky flavor you get from the coals is delicious. You can also add cubes of cheese such as mozzarella or fontina to the skewers.

garlic bread skewers

1 baguette

⅔ cup extra virgin olive oil

2 garlic cloves, crushed

2 tablespoons chopped
fresh flat-leaf parsley

sea salt and freshly ground
black pepper

6–8 wooden skewers,
soaked in water
for 30 minutes

SERVES 6–8

Cut the bread into 1-inch slices, then cut the slices crosswise to make half moons.

Put the olive oil, garlic, parsley, salt, and pepper in a large bowl, add the bread, and toss until well coated with the parsley and oil.

Preheat the grill or stovetop grill pan. Thread the garlic bread onto skewers and cook over medium-hot coals for 2 to 3 minutes on each side until toasted.

VARIATION Cut 8 oz. mozzarella cheese into about 24 small pieces. Thread a piece of bread onto the skewer and continue to alternate the cheese and bread. Cook as in the main recipe.

fish and seafood

Meat and fish (the old-fashioned surf 'n' turf) can work well and this recipe is a perfect example of this balance of strong flavors. I use the chorizo sausage that needs cooking, rather than the cured tapas variety, although either would do.

shrimp, chorizo, and sage skewers

10 oz. uncooked chorizo

24 large uncooked shrimp, peeled and deveined

24 large fresh sage leaves

extra virgin olive oil

freshly squeezed lemon juice

freshly ground black pepper

12 skewers, metal or wooden (if using wooden, soak them in water for 30 minutes)

SERVES 6

Cut the chorizo into 24 slices about ½-inch thick and thread onto the skewers, alternating with the shrimp and sage leaves. Put a little oil and lemon juice in a small bowl or pitcher, mix well, then drizzle over the skewers. Sprinkle with pepper.

Meanwhile, preheat a stovetop grill pan or outdoor grill until hot. Cook the skewers for 1½ to 2 minutes on each side until the chorizo and shrimp are cooked through. Serve at once.

squid piri-piri

Piri-piri, a Portuguese chile condiment traditionally used to baste broiled chicken, is a combination of chopped red chiles, olive oil, and vinegar. It is generally very hot and only a little is needed to add spice to the food. Here I have tempered the heat, but you can use more chiles if you like it spicier. It works very well with squid.

8 medium squid bodies, about 8 oz. each*

freshly squeezed juice of 1 lemon

sea salt

lemon wedges, to serve

PIRI-PIRI SAUCE

8 small red chiles, such as bird's eye

1¼ cups extra virgin olive oil

1 tablespoon white wine vinegar

freshly ground black pepper

16 wooden skewers, soaked in water for 30 minutes

SERVES 4

To prepare the squid, put the squid body on a board and, using a sharp knife, cut down one side and open the tube out flat. Scrape away any remaining insides and wash and dry well.

Skewer each opened-out body with 2 skewers, running them up the long sides of each piece. Rub a little salt over each one and squeeze over the lemon juice. Let marinate in the refrigerator for 30 minutes.

Meanwhile, to make the piri-piri sauce, finely chop the whole chiles without seeding them, and transfer to a small jar or bottle. Add the oil, vinegar, and a little salt and pepper. Shake well and set aside.

Meanwhile, preheat a stovetop grill pan or outdoor grill until hot.

Brush the squid with a small amount of the piri-piri sauce, then cook for 1 to 1½ minutes on each side until charred. Drizzle with extra sauce and serve immediately with lemon wedges.

Note If the squid includes the tentacles, cut them off in one piece, thread with a skewer, and cook and marinate in the same way as the squid bodies.

grilled lobsters with "burnt" butter

I use just the lobster tails for this recipe. If your lobsters have claws, remember to crack them before serving. You can also make this recipe with either langoustines or jumbo shrimp.

6 uncooked lobster tails
or 12 large langoustines
or jumbo shrimp*

2 tablespoons olive oil

1 stick butter

sea salt and freshly ground
black pepper

TO SERVE

lemon wedges

green salad

SERVES 6

Using a very sharp knife, cut the lobster tails in half lengthwise, cutting down through the shell. Brush the flesh with oil and season well with salt and pepper.

Preheat a stovetop grill pan or outdoor grill until medium-hot. Add the lobster tails and cook, shell side down, for about 5 minutes. Brush with more oil and cook, flesh side down, for a further 3 minutes. Remove from the heat and let rest for 5 minutes.

Put the butter in a small saucepan and heat gently until melted and golden. Arrange the lobster tails on a large platter, drizzle with the butter, and squeeze the lemon wedges over the top. Serve with some green salad.

Note If you are using langoustines or shrimp, simply cut them in half and discard the vein running along the back of each one. Cook as above for 2 minutes on each side until cooked through.

grilled fish bathed in oregano and lemon

I have many fond memories of summer holidays in Greece—and none is more prized than the smell of seafood emanating from the dozens of little tavernas dotted along the beach. This is a typical dish of char-grilled bream with oil, oregano, and garlic, but you could use other small fish such as snapper, or even trout.

2 unwaxed lemons

1 cup extra virgin olive oil

1 tablespoon dried oregano

2 garlic cloves, finely chopped

2 tablespoons chopped fresh flat-leaf parsley

6 snapper or bream, about 12 oz. each, well cleaned and scaled

sea salt and freshly ground black pepper

SERVES 6

Grate the zest of 1 lemon into a small bowl and squeeze in the juice. Add ¾ cup oil, the oregano, garlic, parsley, salt, and pepper. Let infuse for at least 1 hour.

Wash and dry the fish inside and out. Using a sharp knife, cut several slashes into each side. Squeeze the juice from the remaining lemon into a bowl, add the remaining ¼ cup oil, salt, and pepper and rub the mixture all over the fish.

Heat the flat plate of an outdoor grill for 10 minutes, add the fish, and cook for 3 to 4 minutes on each side until charred and cooked through. Alternatively, use a stovetop grill pan or large, heavy skillet. Transfer to a warm serving platter, pour over the dressing, and let rest for about 5 minutes before serving.

4 salmon fillets, skinned, about 8 oz. each

sea salt and freshly ground black pepper

CREOLE RUB

½ small onion, finely chopped

1 garlic clove, finely chopped

1 tablespoon chopped fresh thyme

1 tablespoon paprika

1 teaspoon ground cumin

1 teaspoon sea salt

¼ teaspoon cayenne pepper

1 tablespoon brown sugar

MANGO AND SESAME SALSA

1 large ripe mango, peeled, pitted, and chopped

4 scallions, chopped

1 fresh hot red chile, seeded and chopped

1 garlic clove, crushed

1 tablespoon light soy sauce

1 tablespoon freshly squeezed lime juice

1 teaspoon sesame oil

½ tablespoon sugar

1 tablespoon chopped fresh cilantro

a large handful of wood chips, such as hickory, soaked in water for 1 hour, drained

SERVES 4

Smoking food on the grill is simply magical—the flavors are truly wonderful. You will need a grill with a lid for this recipe. If you have a gas grill, follow the manufacturer's instructions for indirect grill-smoking.

hot-smoked **creole salmon**

To make the Creole rub, put all the ingredients in a small bowl and stir well.

Wash the salmon under cold running water and pat dry with paper towels. Using tweezers, pull out any bones, then put the fish in a dish and work the Creole rub all over it. Cover and let marinate in the refrigerator for at least 1 hour.

To make the salsa, put the chopped mango in a bowl and add the scallions, chile, garlic, soy sauce, lime juice, sesame oil, sugar, cilantro, salt, and pepper. Mix well and set aside for 30 minutes to let the flavors infuse.

Preheat the charcoal grill. When the coals are hot, rake them into 2 piles at either side of the grill and put a foil drip tray in the middle. Tip half the soaked wood chips onto each pile of coals. Cover with the lid, keeping any air vents open during cooking.

As soon as the wood chips start to smoke, put the salmon fillets in the center of the grill, cover, and cook for 15 to 20 minutes or until the salmon is cooked.

To test the fish, press the salmon with your finger—the flesh should feel firm and start to open into flakes. Serve hot or cold with the mango and sesame salsa.

A great way to prepare whole salmon is to remove the central bone from the fish, then tie the two fillets back together. If your filleting skills are limited, just ask your friendly fishseller to fillet the whole fish for you.

whole salmon stuffed with herbs

Put the salmon fillets flat on a board, flesh side up. Carefully pull out any remaining bones with tweezers.

Put the butter, herbs, lemon zest, garlic, and plenty of pepper in a small bowl and beat well. Spread the mixture over one of the salmon fillets and put the second on the top, arranging them top to tail.

Using kitchen twine, tie the fish together at 1-inch intervals. Brush with a little oil, sprinkle with salt and pepper, and cook on the flat plate of an outdoor grill for 10 minutes on each side. Remove the salmon from the heat and let rest for 10 minutes. Remove the twine and serve the fish cut into portions.

4 lb. whole salmon, filleted

1 stick butter, softened

1 cup chopped fresh mixed soft-leaf herbs, such as basil, chives, mint, parsley, and tarragon

grated zest of 1 unwaxed lemon

1 garlic clove, crushed

sea salt and freshly ground black pepper

olive oil, for brushing

kitchen twine

SERVES 8

1½ lb. swordfish, tuna, or mahi-mahi steaks

extra virgin olive oil

24 large bay leaves, soaked in cold water for 1 hour

2 lemons, cut into 24 chunks

freshly squeezed lemon juice

MOROCCAN RUB

½ tablespoon coriander seeds

½ teaspoon cumin seeds

1 cinnamon stick

½ teaspoon whole allspice berries

6 cloves

a pinch of saffron threads

½ teaspoon ground turmeric

1 teaspoon dried onion flakes

½ teaspoon sea salt

¼ teaspoon paprika

COUSCOUS

10 oz. couscous, 1½ cups

1¼ cups boiling water

2 oz. freshly grated Parmesan cheese, ½ cup

4 tablespoons butter, melted

1 tablespoon chopped fresh thyme leaves

sea salt and freshly ground black pepper

8 wooden skewers, soaked in water for 30 minutes

SERVES 4

Chunks of swordfish coated in a spicy rub, then grilled on skewers and served with fluffy couscous make the perfect lunch. Chicken would also work well in this recipe.

moroccan fish skewers
with couscous

To make the Moroccan rub, toast the whole spices and saffron threads in a dry skillet over medium heat for 1 to 2 minutes or until golden and aromatic. Remove from the heat and let cool. Transfer to a spice grinder (or clean coffee grinder) and crush to a coarse powder. Alternatively, use a mortar and pestle. Put the spices in a bowl, add the remaining ingredients, and mix well.

Using a sharp knife, cut the swordfish into 32 cubes and put them in a shallow ceramic dish. Add a sprinkle of olive oil and the Moroccan rub and toss well until the fish is evenly coated. Cover and let marinate in the refrigerator for 1 hour.

About 10 minutes before cooking the fish, put the couscous in a heatproof bowl and pour over 1¼ cups boiling water. Let plump for a few minutes, then fluff with a fork. Transfer the couscous to a warmed serving dish and immediately stir in the Parmesan cheese, melted butter, thyme, salt, and pepper. Keep the couscous warm.

Meanwhile, preheat the grill or stovetop grill pan. Thread the fish, bay leaves, and chunks of lemon onto the soaked skewers and cook over hot coals for 3 to 4 minutes, turning half-way through, until cooked. Serve the skewers on a bed of couscous, sprinkled with a little olive oil and lemon juice.

peppered tuna steak
with salsa rossa

⅓ cup mixed peppercorns, coarsely crushed

6 tuna steaks, 8 oz. each

1 tablespoon extra virgin olive oil

mixed salad leaves, to serve

SALSA ROSSA

1 large red bell pepper

1 tablespoon extra virgin olive oil

2 garlic cloves, crushed

2 large ripe tomatoes, peeled and coarsely chopped

a small pinch of hot red pepper flakes

1 tablespoon dried oregano

1 tablespoon red wine vinegar

sea salt and freshly ground black pepper

SERVES 6

Salsa rossa is one of those divine Italian sauces that transforms simple meat and fish dishes into food nirvana. The slight sweetness from the peppers is a good foil for the spicy pepper crust.

To make the salsa rossa, broil the pepper until charred all over, then put in a plastic bag and let cool. Remove and discard the skin and seeds, reserving any juices, then chop the flesh.

Put the oil in a skillet, heat gently, then add the garlic and sauté for 3 minutes. Add the tomatoes, pepper flakes, and oregano and simmer gently for 15 minutes. Stir in the chopped peppers and the vinegar and simmer for a further 5 minutes to evaporate any excess liquid.

Transfer the mixture to a blender and purée until fairly smooth. Add salt and pepper to taste and let cool. The salsa may be stored in a screw-top jar in the refrigerator for up to 3 days.

Put the crushed peppercorns on a large plate. Brush the tuna steaks with oil, then press the crushed peppercorns into the surface. Preheat a stovetop grill pan or outdoor grill until hot, add the tuna, and cook for 1 minute on each side. Wrap loosely in foil and let rest for 5 minutes before serving with the salsa rossa and a salad of mixed leaves.

I love to serve this dish whenever I see some really fresh swordfish at the market. It is easy to overcook swordfish, which will become tough, so follow the timings below and err on the side of caution—you can always put the fish back on the heat for a moment or two longer if necessary.

seared swordfish
with new potatoes, beans, and olives

Brush the swordfish steaks with 1 tablespoon of the oil, season with salt and pepper, and set aside.

To make the dressing, put the remaining oil in a bowl, add the lemon juice, sugar, chives, salt, and pepper, beat well, and set aside.

Cook the potatoes in a saucepan of lightly salted boiling water for 10 minutes, add the beans, and cook for a further 3 to 4 minutes or until the potatoes and beans are just tender. Drain well, add the olives and half the dressing, and toss well.

Cook the swordfish steaks on a preheated outdoor grill or stovetop grill pan for about 1½ minutes on each side. Wrap loosely in foil and let rest for 5 minutes, then serve with the warm potato and bean salad, sprinkled with the remaining dressing and balsamic vinegar.

Note To reduce balsamic vinegar, put 1¼ cups vinegar in a small saucepan and boil gently until it is reduced by two-thirds and reaches the consistency of thick syrup. Let cool, then store in a clean bottle.

4 swordfish, tuna, or mahi-mahi steaks, 8 oz. each

½ cup extra virgin olive oil

2 tablespoons freshly squeezed lemon juice

½ teaspoon sugar

1 tablespoon chopped fresh chives

1 lb. new potatoes, cut in half if large

8 oz. string beans, trimmed

2 oz. black olives, such as Niçoise or Kalamata, pitted and chopped, about ½ cup

sea salt and freshly ground black pepper

reduced balsamic vinegar, to serve*

SERVES 4

poultry

12 chicken wings

2 tablespoons extra virgin olive oil

1 tablespoon jerk seasoning powder or 2 tablespoons paste*

freshly squeezed juice of ½ lemon

1 teaspoon sea salt

AVOCADO SALSA

1 large ripe avocado

2 ripe tomatoes, peeled, seeded, and chopped

1 garlic clove, crushed

1 small red chile, seeded and chopped

freshly squeezed juice of ½ lemon

2 tablespoons chopped fresh cilantro

1 tablespoon extra virgin olive oil

sea salt and freshly ground black pepper

SERVES 4

Jerk seasoning is Jamaica's popular spice mix, used to spark up meat, poultry, and fish, especially the delicious barbecued offerings sold at the roadside jerk huts so beloved of tourists and locals alike. The seasoning is a combination of allspice, cinnamon, chile, nutmeg, thyme, and sugar and is available in powder or paste form from larger supermarkets and specialty food stores.

jerk chicken wings with avocado salsa

Put the chicken wings in a ceramic dish. Mix the oil, jerk seasoning, lemon juice, and salt in a bowl, pour over the wings, and stir well to coat. Cover and let marinate in the refrigerator overnight.

The next day cook the wings either on a preheated outdoor grill or under a hot broiler for 5 to 6 minutes on each side, basting occasionally with any remaining marinade until charred and tender.

To make the salsa, put all the ingredients in a bowl, mix well, and season to taste with salt and pepper. Serve the wings with the salsa.

Note If you don't have any jerk seasoning on hand, try another spice mix or spice paste instead. Just remember, jerk is very fiery indeed, so you need a spicy one.

Skewering and marinating small pieces of meat to grill over hot coals is something of a passion in Morocco. Braziers can be found on many street corners, the delicious smells of their cooking tempting hungry passers-by.

chicken kabobs moroccan-style

Cut the chicken lengthwise into ⅛-inch strips and put in a shallow, non-metal dish. Put the oil, lemon juice, thyme, garlic, turmeric, cinnamon, allspice, salt, and cayenne pepper in a pitcher, mix well, then pour over the chicken strips. Cover well and let marinate in the refrigerator overnight.

The next day, return the chicken to room temperature for 1 hour. Thread the strips onto skewers, zigzagging back and forth. Cook on a preheated outdoor grill or stovetop grill pan for 3 to 4 minutes on each side until charred and cooked through. Serve with lemon wedges and yogurt.

1 lb. skinless chicken breast fillets

2 tablespoons extra virgin olive oil

freshly squeezed juice of 1 large lemon

1 tablespoon chopped fresh thyme leaves

2 garlic cloves, crushed

1 teaspoon ground turmeric

1 teaspoon ground cinnamon

½ teaspoon ground allspice

½ teaspoon sea salt

¼ teaspoon ground cayenne pepper

TO SERVE

lemon wedges

plain yogurt

8 wooden skewers, soaked in water for 30 minutes

SERVES 4

This delicious concoction of olives, lemons, fresh marjoram, and succulent chicken makes an ideal entrée for a casual backyard barbecue. Serve with a selection of salads, such as tomato and basil.

olive-infused **chicken**

1 chicken, 3 lb.

3 oz. black olives, such as Niçoise, pitted

¼ cup extra virgin olive oil

1 teaspoon sea salt

2 tablespoons chopped fresh marjoram

freshly squeezed juice of 1 lemon

freshly ground black pepper

2 lemons, cut in half, to serve

SERVES 4

To prepare the chicken, put it on a board with the back facing upwards and, using kitchen shears, cut along each side of the backbone and remove it completely. Using your fingers, gently ease the skin away from the flesh, taking care not to tear the skin, then put the chicken in a large, shallow dish. Put the olives, olive oil, salt, marjoram, and lemon juice in a separate bowl and mix well, then pour over the chicken and push as many of the olives as possible between the skin and flesh of the chicken. Cover and let marinate in the refrigerator for 2 hours.

Preheat the grill, then cook the chicken cut side down over medium-hot coals for 15 minutes. Using tongs, turn the chicken over and cook for a further 10 minutes until the skin is charred, the flesh is cooked through, and the juices run clear when the thickest part of the meat is pierced with a skewer.

Let the chicken rest for 10 minutes before cutting into 4 pieces and serving with the lemon halves.

2 red bell peppers,
left whole

4 small focaccia or Turkish
rolls, cut in half

2 large, cooked chicken
breasts, shredded into
long pieces

a small handful of
baby spinach

ARUGULA AÏOLI

1 egg yolk

1 teaspoon white
wine vinegar

a bunch of arugula, about
2 oz., coarsely chopped

1 garlic clove, crushed

⅔ cup olive oil

sea salt and freshly ground
black pepper

SERVES 4

Panini, which is Italian for "toasted sandwiches," can be assembled in advance, then cooked just before you want to serve them. The combination of grilled bell peppers, tender chicken, and a delicious arugula aïoli is definitely hard to beat.

chicken panini
with roasted pepper and arugula aïoli

Preheat the grill, then cook the peppers over hot coals or under a preheated broiler for about 20 minutes until charred all over. Put in a plastic bag, seal, and let cool. Peel the peppers, discard the seeds, then cut the flesh into strips.

To make the aïoli, put the egg yolk, vinegar, and a little salt and pepper in a food processor and blend briefly until frothy. Add the arugula and garlic and pulse for 30 seconds. With the machine still running, gradually pour in the olive oil until the sauce is thickened and speckled vividly green. Taste and adjust the seasoning with salt and pepper, if necessary.

Spread a little of the arugula aïoli onto the cut sides of each roll and fill the rolls with the chicken, pepper strips, and spinach leaves. Press the halves together.

Preheat the flat plate on the grill and cook the panini over low heat for 4 to 5 minutes, then, using tongs, flip over and cook the second side for a further 5 minutes until toasted. If you don't have a flat plate, cook on a cast-iron griddle, either on the grill, or on the stove. Serve hot.

grilled mexican-style **cornish hens**

Butterflied Cornish hens are ideally suited to grilling, as the process of opening them out flat ensures quick and even cooking. The marinade ingredients have a Mexican flavor and work particularly well accompanied by the Creamy Corn Salsa on page 95.

4 Cornish game hens

Creamy Corn Salsa, to serve (page 95)

MEXICAN MARINADE

4 jalapeño chiles

8 garlic cloves

¼ cup orange juice

2 tablespoons freshly squeezed lime juice

1 tablespoon ground cumin

1 tablespoon dried oregano or thyme

2 teaspoons sea salt

⅓ cup olive oil

1 tablespoon maple syrup or honey

SERVES 4

To butterfly the hens, turn them breast side down on a board and, using poultry shears or sturdy kitchen shears, cut down each side of the backbone and discard it. Turn the birds over and open them out flat, pressing down hard on the breastbone. Thread 2 skewers diagonally through each hen from the wings to the thigh bones.

To make the marinade, skewer the chiles and garlic together and cook on a preheated medium-hot outdoor grill or under a broiler for 10 minutes, turning frequently, until evenly browned. Scrape off and discard the skins from the chiles and chop the flesh coarsely. Put the flesh and seeds in a blender, add the garlic and all the remaining marinade ingredients, and blend to a purée.

Pour the marinade over the hens, cover, and let marinate in the refrigerator overnight. Return them to room temperature for 1 hour before cooking

When ready to cook, remove the birds from the marinade and grill over preheated medium-hot coals for 12 minutes on each side, basting occasionally. Remove from the heat, let rest for 5 minutes, then serve with the creamy corn salsa.

I love the simplicity of Japanese cooking, where just a few strong flavors combine perfectly. The cucumber salad, borrowed from Thai cuisine, cuts through the richness of the duck and its delicious glaze.

duck yakitori

Put the soy sauce, sake, and sugar in a small saucepan and heat gently to dissolve the sugar. Remove from the heat and let cool completely.

Cut the duck lengthwise into ⅛-inch strips and put in a shallow dish. Pour over the soy sauce mixture, cover, and let marinate in the refrigerator for 2 to 4 hours or preferably overnight.

Just before cooking the duck, prepare the salad. Put the vinegar, sugar, and 2 tablespoons water in a small saucepan, heat to dissolve the sugar, then let cool. Stir in the cucumber and chile and set aside.

Thread the duck strips onto skewers, zigzagging back and forth. Cook on a preheated outdoor grill or under a broiler for 2 minutes on each side until cooked through. Serve with chilled soba noodles and the cucumber salad.

⅓ cup Japanese soy sauce

3 tablespoons sake

2 tablespoons sugar

4 small duck breast fillets, about 5 oz. each, skinned

soba noodles, cooked according to the package instructions, then drained and chilled, to serve

CUCUMBER SALAD

2 tablespoons rice vinegar

2 tablespoons sugar

½ cucumber, about 8 inches, thinly sliced

1 fresh hot red chile, such as serrano, seeded and chopped

8 wooden skewers, soaked in water for 30 minutes

SERVES 4

This dish is similar to the famous Peking duck but minus the time it takes to prepare it! Cooking duck on an outdoor grill is best done by the indirect grilling method (page 43) where the coals are pushed to the sides and a drip tray placed underneath to catch the fat.

barbecue duck rice paper rolls

2 duck breast fillets, with skin, about 8 oz. each

1 tablespoon sea salt

2 tablespoons honey

2 tablespoons dark soy sauce

½ teaspoon ground star anise

1 package Vietnamese rice paper wrappers (*bahn trang*)*

½ cucumber, cut into strips

a few fresh herb leaves, such as cilantro, mint, and Thai basil

ASIAN BARBECUE SAUCE

½ cup crushed tomatoes

2 tablespoons hoisin sauce

1 teaspoon hot chile sauce

2 garlic cloves, crushed

2 tablespoons sweet soy sauce

1 tablespoon rice wine vinegar

1 teaspoon ground coriander

½ teaspoon ground cinnamon

¼ teaspoon Chinese five-spice pepper

SERVES 4

Using a sharp knife, cut several slashes into the duck skin. Rub the skin with the salt and put in a shallow dish. Put the honey, soy sauce, and ground star anise in a bowl and mix well. Pour over the duck. Cover and let marinate in the refrigerator for at least 1 hour.

To make the Asian barbecue sauce, mix all the ingredients in a small saucepan, add ½ cup water, bring to a boil, and simmer gently for 10 minutes. Remove from the heat and let cool.

Set up the grill for indirect grilling (page 43) and put a drip tray in the middle. Cook the duck breast for 15 minutes or until well browned and firm to the touch, let rest for 5 minutes, then cut into thin strips and set aside until ready to serve.

Put the rice paper wrappers in a large bowl of cold water, let soak until softened, then pat dry and spread flat on the work surface. Put a few slices of duck, some strips of cucumber, and herbs in the center of each one and add a little of the Asian barbecue sauce.

Fold the ends of the wrapper over the duck and roll up the sides to enclose the filling. Transfer to a large platter and serve with the Asian barbecue sauce.

Note Rice paper wrappers are sold in packages of 50 or 100. Seal leftovers in the same package, put in a plastic bag, and seal well.

meat

Buy the best hot dogs you can find. Those packed in natural casings are usually very good, especially with the caramelized onions and whole-grain mustard in this recipe.

top dogs

2 onions, cut into thin wedges

2–3 tablespoons extra virgin olive oil

1 tablespoon chopped fresh sage leaves

4 natural casing frankfurters
or bratwursts, pricked

4 hot dog buns

4 tablespoons whole-grain mustard

2 ripe tomatoes, sliced

sea salt and freshly ground black pepper

Barbecue Sauce (page 95),
to serve (optional)

SERVES 4

Put the onion wedges in a bowl, add the olive oil, sage, and a little salt and pepper, and mix well. Preheat the flat plate on the gas grill and cook the onions for 15 to 20 minutes, stirring occasionally until golden and tender. If you have a charcoal grill, cook the onions in a skillet on the grill. Alternatively, cook them on a preheated stovetop grill pan. Keep the onions hot.

Meanwhile, cook the frankfurters or bratwursts over hot coals or on a preheated stovetop grill pan for 10 to 12 minutes, turning frequently until browned and cooked through. Transfer to a plate and let rest briefly.

Cut the buns almost in half, then put on the grill rack or stovetop grill pan and toast for a few minutes. Remove from the heat and spread with mustard. Fill with the tomatoes, sausages, and onions. Add a little barbecue sauce, if using, and serve.

Although pork should not be served rare, it is quite easy to overcook it, leaving the meat dry and tough. A good test is to pierce the meat with a skewer, leave it there for a second, remove it, and carefully feel how hot it is—it should feel warm, not too hot or too cold, for the perfect result.

2 tablespoons chopped fresh sage leaves

2 tablespoons whole-grain mustard

2 tablespoons extra virgin olive oil

4 large pork chops

sea salt and freshly ground black pepper

SMOKY TOMATO SALSA

4 ripe plum tomatoes

2 fresh hot red chiles, about 2 inches long, seeded and chopped

4 whole garlic cloves, peeled

1 red onion, quartered

¼ cup extra virgin olive oil

1 tablespoon freshly squeezed lemon juice

2 tablespoons chopped fresh cilantro

sea salt and freshly ground black pepper

2 wooden skewers, soaked in water for 30 minutes

SERVES 4

sage-rubbed **pork chops**

To make the tomato salsa, hold the tomatoes over the flames of the grill with tongs for about 1 minute, turning frequently, until the skin is charred all over. Alternatively, cook the tomatoes on a preheated stovetop grill pan, turning frequently, until charred all over. Let cool, peel, cut in half, remove and discard the seeds, then chop the flesh. Repeat with the chiles.

Thread the garlic cloves and onion quarters onto separate skewers. Cook the garlic over hot coals for 3 to 4 minutes and the onion for 10 to 12 minutes until they are charred and softened. Let cool, remove from the skewers, and cut into cubes.

Put the tomatoes, chiles, garlic, and onion in a bowl and stir in the oil, lemon juice, and cilantro. Season to taste with salt and pepper. Cover and store in the refrigerator until required.

Put the sage, mustard, and oil in a bowl and mix well. Season with a little salt and pepper, then spread the mixture all over the chops. Cover and let marinate in the refrigerator for 1 hour.

Preheat the grill, then cook the chops over hot coals for 2½ to 3 minutes on each side until browned and cooked through. Alternatively, cook the chops on a preheated hot stovetop grill pan. Serve hot with the tomato salsa.

These grilled ribs are spicy, smoky, sticky, tender, and lip-smackingly good. They may take a little time to prepare because of soaking and marinating, but they are simple to cook and definitely well worth the effort.

smoky **spareribs**

2½ lb. spareribs

1¼ cups white wine vinegar

2 tablespoons brown sugar

1 tablespoon sea salt

1 tablespoon sweet paprika

2 teaspoons crushed black pepper

2 teaspoons onion powder

1 teaspoon garlic powder

¼ teaspoon cayenne pepper

⅔ cup Barbecue Sauce (page 95)

Creamy Coleslaw (page 94), to serve

SERVES 4

Wash the spareribs under cold running water and pat dry with paper towels. Put the spareribs in a large dish, add the vinegar, and let soak for 4 hours or overnight. Rinse the ribs well and pat dry with paper towels.

Put the sugar, salt, paprika, pepper, onion powder, garlic powder, and cayenne in a bowl and mix well. Rub the mixture all over the spareribs, cover, and let marinate in the refrigerator for 2 hours.

Preheat the grill, then cook the spareribs over low heat for 20 minutes on each side. Brush with the barbecue sauce and cook for a further 15 minutes on each side until the ribs are lightly charred, tender, and sticky. Remove and let cool briefly, then serve with the coleslaw.

best-ever **beef burger**

1 ½ lb. ground sirloin

2 oz. ground pork (not too lean)

8 anchovy fillets in oil, drained and finely chopped

1 cup soft white bread crumbs

2 tablespoons chopped fresh thyme

1 tablespoon whole-grain mustard

1 large egg, lightly beaten

sea salt and freshly ground black pepper

TO SERVE

hamburger buns

sautéed onions

dill pickles

tomato, lettuce, and olive salad (optional)

SERVES 6

There are many burger recipes and everyone has their favorite—this one is very good. I always serve it in a bun, with pickles and sauce, and a simple salad of tomatoes, lettuce, and olives.

Put the ground sirloin and pork in a bowl and add the anchovies, bread crumbs, thyme, mustard, beaten egg, salt, and pepper, working the ingredients with your hands to make a nice, sticky mixture.

Shape into 6 even-size burgers, cover, and chill in the refrigerator for 1 hour. Cook on a preheated outdoor grill, on a stovetop grill pan, or in a lightly oiled skillet for about 4 minutes on each side. Remove from the heat and let rest for 5 minutes. Serve in a bun, with sautéed onions, dill pickles, and the tomato, lettuce, and olive salad, if using.

If you can find porcini mushrooms all the better, but any large open mushroom such as portobello will taste great cooked on the grill.

peppered beef
tenderloin with mushrooms

Brush the beef with the olive oil, press the peppercorns into the meat, then sprinkle with salt.

Preheat the grill to high or a stovetop grill pan until hot. Cook the beef, turning every 5 minutes or so, until evenly browned on all sides. Cook for 15 minutes for rare, 20 minutes for medium, and 25 minutes for well done. Transfer the beef to a roasting pan, cover with foil, and let rest for 10 minutes.

Brush the mushrooms with olive oil, season with salt and pepper, then put them stem side down on the grill rack or stovetop grill pan and cook for 5 minutes on each side. Transfer to the roasting pan and let rest for 1 to 2 minutes.

Meanwhile, put all the dressing ingredients in a bowl and mix well. Serve the beef in thick slices with the mushrooms and a sprinkle of the dressing.

1 lb. beef tenderloin

1 tablespoon extra virgin olive oil, plus extra for brushing

1 tablespoon crushed black peppercorns

8 large porcini or portobello mushrooms

sea salt and freshly ground black pepper

DRESSING

½ cup extra virgin olive oil

1 garlic clove, chopped

1 tablespoon chopped fresh parsley

a squeeze of fresh lemon juice

SERVES 4

pan-grilled vietnamese beef
with sour cream and chile tomato relish

This combination of Vietnamese marinated beef, sour cream, steamed sweet potatoes, and spicy chile tomato relish makes a terrific party piece.

To make the chile tomato relish, put all the ingredients in a food processor and pulse until coarsely chopped. Transfer to a saucepan, bring to a boil, skim off the foam, then reduce the heat and simmer for 30 minutes. Remove from the heat, set aside, and let cool.

Put the marinade ingredients in a shallow dish and mix well. Add the beef, cover, and set aside for at least 15 minutes. Turn the beef over and let marinate for at least another 15 minutes. Alternatively, let marinate in the refrigerator overnight.

Heat a stovetop grill pan to medium-hot. Add the beef and cook for about 2 minutes on each side. The meat should be brown outside and rare in the middle. If you want it medium, cook for another 2 minutes.

Meanwhile, steam the sweet potatoes until a fork pierces them easily. Alternatively, boil in salted water, then drain.

To serve, put a handful of salad greens on each plate, add a steak and a scoop of sweet potatoes, then a spoonful of sour cream and 1 to 2 tablespoons chile tomato relish.

4 slices of beef tenderloin steak, 1-inch thick, about 1 lb.

4 small orange-fleshed sweet potatoes, peeled and cut crosswise into 1-inch slices

MARINADE

2 tablespoons fish sauce

2 tablespoons mirin (Japanese sweet rice wine)

1 tablespoon toasted sesame oil

grated zest and juice of 1 unwaxed lime

CHILE TOMATO RELISH

4 ripe plum tomatoes, peeled and chopped

3 red bell peppers, peeled and chopped

6 red jalapeño chiles, seeded and chopped

3-inch piece of fresh ginger, peeled and grated

2 tablespoons sea salt

1 cup sugar

⅓ cup sherry vinegar

TO SERVE

a few handfuls of salad greens

4 heaping tablespoons sour cream

SERVES 4

thai-style **beef salad**

1 tablespoon Szechuan peppercorns, or black peppercorns, lightly crushed

1 teaspoon ground coriander

1 teaspoon sea salt

1 lb. beef fillet, in one piece

1 tablespoon peanut or canola oil

1 cucumber, thinly sliced

4 scallions, thinly sliced

2 baby bok choy, thinly sliced

a handful of fresh Thai basil leaves

a handful of fresh mint leaves

a handful of fresh cilantro

LIME DRESSING

1 tablespoon palm sugar or brown sugar

1 tablespoon Thai fish sauce (*nam pla*)

2 tablespoons freshly squeezed lime juice

2 small fresh hot red chiles, such as bird's eye, seeded and chopped

1 garlic clove, crushed

SERVES 4

What I love about many Thai dishes (as well as Vietnamese and Indonesian) is their use of fresh herbs. Many of their salads, soups, and stews are flooded with the pungent flavors of Thai basil, mint, and cilantro. Thai basil is available from Asian stores, but you could use regular basil instead. Bok choy is also known as "pak choi" in some places.

Put the peppercorns, coriander, and salt on a plate and mix. Rub the beef all over with the oil and then put onto the plate and turn to coat with the spices.

Cook the beef on a preheated outdoor grill or stovetop grill pan for about 10 minutes, turning to brown evenly. Remove from the heat and let cool.

Meanwhile, to make the dressing, put the sugar in a saucepan, add the fish sauce and 2 tablespoons water, and heat until the sugar dissolves. Let cool, then stir in the lime juice, chiles, and garlic.

Cut the beef into thin slices and put in a large bowl. Add the cucumber, scallions, bok choy, and herbs. Pour over the dressing, toss well, then serve.

butterflied lamb with indian spices

"Butterfly" is the term used when a piece of meat or fish is opened out flat. When preparing a leg of lamb, the bone is removed so the meat can be laid out flat, so it will cook quickly and evenly. It's easy to do, but you can also ask your butcher to do it for you. Serve the lamb with Indian breads such as naan or chapattis, or with pita bread.

To butterfly the lamb, turn to the side of the leg where the bone is closest to the surface. Using a sharp knife, cut down the length of the bone, then run your knife close to the bone, using small cuts, to separate the bone from the flesh. Remove and discard the bone. Open out the butterflied lamb and cut several shallow slashes in each side.

Put the onion, garlic, and ginger in a blender and process to a smooth paste. Transfer to a medium bowl and set aside.

Put the cinnamon stick, coriander and cumin seeds, and cloves in a dry skillet and heat gently until lightly browned and aromatic. Let cool slightly, then grind to a powder in a spice grinder or with a mortar and pestle. Add to the onion paste, then stir in the curry powder, tomato purée, oil, salt, and pepper.

Spread this paste all over the lamb, cover, and let marinate overnight in the refrigerator. Return the lamb to room temperature for about 1 hour before cooking.

When ready to cook, scrape off the excess marinade, brush the lamb with a little oil, and put on the grill rack over medium-hot coals. Cook for 12 to 15 minutes on each side until the outside is charred (leaving the center beautifully pink). Remove the lamb from the heat and let it rest for 10 minutes before carving.

Serve the lamb with Indian breads, plain yogurt, and a few sprigs of cilantro.

3 lb. leg of lamb, butterflied

1 onion, chopped

4 garlic cloves, chopped

1 tablespoon grated fresh ginger

1 cinnamon stick, coarsely crumbled

1 tablespoon coriander seeds

2 teaspoons cumin seeds

¼ teaspoon whole cloves

1 tablespoon curry powder

2 tablespoons tomato purée

2 tablespoons peanut or canola oil, plus extra for brushing

sea salt and freshly ground black pepper

TO SERVE

Indian breads

plain yogurt

sprigs of cilantro

SERVES 6–8

The classic Greek kabob, called "souvlaki," is a delicious combination of cubed lamb marinated in red wine with herbs and lemon juice. The meat is tenderized by the wine, resulting in a juicy, succulent dish.

kabobs with cracked wheat salad

Trim any large pieces of fat from the lamb, then cut the meat into 1-inch cubes. Put in a shallow, non-metal dish. Add the rosemary, oregano, onion, garlic, wine, lemon juice, olive oil, salt, and pepper. Toss well, cover, and let marinate in the refrigerator for 4 hours. Return to room temperature for 1 hour before cooking.

To make the salad, soak the cracked wheat in warm water for 30 minutes until the water is absorbed and the grains have softened. Strain well to extract any excess water and transfer the wheat to a bowl. Add all the remaining ingredients, season to taste with salt and pepper, and set aside for 30 minutes to develop the flavors.

Thread the lamb onto large rosemary stalks or metal skewers. Cook on a preheated outdoor grill or under a broiler for 10 minutes, turning and basting from time to time. Let rest for 5 minutes, then serve with the salad.

2 lb. boneless lamb, such as shoulder

1 tablespoon chopped fresh rosemary, plus 6 large stalks, for skewering, if using

1 tablespoon dried oregano

1 onion, chopped

4 garlic cloves, chopped

1¼ cups red wine

freshly squeezed juice of 1 lemon

⅓ cup olive oil

sea salt and freshly ground black pepper

CRACKED WHEAT SALAD

3¼ cups cracked wheat (bulghur wheat)

1 cup chopped fresh flat-leaf parsley

½ cup fresh mint leaves

2 garlic cloves, crushed

½ cup extra virgin olive oil

freshly squeezed juice of 2 lemons

a pinch of sugar

6 metal skewers (optional)

SERVES 6

desserts

grilled pears with spiced honey, walnuts, and gorgonzola

A simple but delicious dessert—the pears, blue cheese, and walnuts perfectly complement each other. Serve on toast with a glass or two of dessert wine. For the best results, choose ripe but firm pears.

Put the walnuts in a skillet, add the honey and cardamom, and cook over high heat until the honey bubbles furiously and starts to darken. Immediately pour the mixture onto a sheet of wax paper and let cool.

Peel the nuts from the paper and set aside.

Preheat the grill. Using a sharp knife, cut the pears into quarters and remove and discard the cores. Cut the pear quarters into thick wedges. Dust lightly with sugar and cook over medium-hot coals for 1½ minutes on each side.

Pile the pears onto slices of toast, sprinkle with the walnuts, and serve with some Gorgonzola cheese and a glass of dessert wine.

2 oz. walnuts

2 tablespoons honey

¼ teaspoon ground cardamom

4 pears

2 tablespoons sugar

4 oz. Gorgonzola cheese

TO SERVE

toast

dessert wine

wax paper

SERVES 4

Toasting the dried coconut enriches the ice cream and gives it a lovely nutty flavor. Although in this recipe I serve it with wedges of grilled pineapple, it works equally well with other fruits such as mangoes or peaches.

toasted coconut ice cream
with grilled pineapple

1 pineapple, medium or small, with leafy top if possible

½ cup brown sugar

1 stick unsalted butter

⅓ cup dark rum

ICE CREAM

⅓ cup dried unsweetened shredded coconut

1¾ cups heavy cream

1¼ cups coconut milk

½ cup sugar

5 egg yolks

an ice cream maker (optional)

SERVES 6

To make the ice cream, put the shredded coconut in a dry skillet and toast, stirring over medium heat for 2 to 3 minutes until evenly browned. Transfer to a saucepan, then add the cream, coconut milk, and sugar. Heat gently until it just reaches boiling point.

Put the egg yolks in a bowl and beat with a wooden spoon until pale. Stir in about 2 tablespoons of the hot custard, then return the mixture to the pan. Heat gently, stirring constantly, until the mixture thickens enough to coat the back of the wooden spoon. Remove the pan from the heat and let cool completely.

When cold, strain the custard, and freeze in an ice cream maker according to the manufacturer's instructions. Transfer to the freezer until required. Alternatively, pour the cold custard into a plastic container and freeze for 5 hours, beating at hourly intervals with a balloon whisk to break up the ice crystals.

To prepare the pineapple, cut it lengthwise into wedges (including the leafy top) and remove the core sections. Put the sugar, butter, and rum in a small saucepan and heat until the sugar dissolves. Brush a little of the mixture over the pineapple wedges, then cook them on a preheated outdoor grill or on a stovetop grill pan for 2 minutes on each side until charred and tender. Remove from the heat and, holding the flesh with a fork, cut between the skin and flesh with a sharp knife. Cut the flesh into segments to make it easier to eat, then reassemble the wedges. Serve with the ice cream and remaining rum sauce, about 2 tablespoons each.

Wrapping fruits in foil is a great way to cook them on the grill—all the juices are contained in the package while the fruit softens.

grilled fruit packages

Put the fruit in a large bowl, add the orange juice, cinnamon, and sugar, and mix well. Divide the fruit mixture between 4 sheets of foil. Fold the foil over the fruit and seal the edges to make packages.

Mix the yogurt, cream, honey, and rose water in a separate bowl. Set aside until needed.

Preheat the grill, then cook the packages over medium-hot coals for 5 to 6 minutes. Remove the packages from the heat, open carefully, and transfer to 4 serving bowls. Serve with the yogurt and a sprinkling of pistachio nuts.

4 peaches or nectarines, cut in half, pitted, and sliced

8 oz. blueberries, 1½ cups

4 oz. raspberries, ¾ cup

freshly squeezed juice of 1 orange

1 teaspoon ground cinnamon

2 tablespoons sugar

1 cup plain yogurt

2 tablespoons heavy cream

1 tablespoon honey

1 tablespoon rose water

1 tablespoon chopped pistachios

SERVES 4

Figs are delicious grilled, but this dish would work equally well with any type of stone fruit, such as plums, peaches, or nectarines.

grilled figs with almond mascarpone cream

6 oz. mascarpone cheese

½ teaspoon pure vanilla extract

1 tablespoon toasted ground almonds, or slivered almonds crushed to a powder with a mortar and pestle

1 tablespoon Marsala wine

1 tablespoon honey

1 tablespoon sugar

1 teaspoon ground cardamom

8–10 figs, cut in half

SERVES 4

Put the mascarpone cheese, vanilla, almonds, Marsala, and honey in a bowl and beat well. Cover and set aside in the refrigerator until needed.

Mix the sugar and ground cardamom in a separate bowl, then carefully dip the cut surface of the figs in the mixture.

Preheat the grill, then cook the figs over medium-hot coals for 1 to 2 minutes on each side until charred and softened. Alternatively, cook the figs on a preheated stovetop grill pan. Transfer the grilled figs to 4 serving bowls and serve with the almond mascarpone cream.

Here's one for the kids, and for adults who remember being kids. I prefer to use sweet cookies, such as langue du chat or almond thins instead of graham crackers, but any will do.

s'mores

16 cookies

8 squares of plain chocolate

16 marshmallows

8 metal skewers

SERVES 4

Put half the cookies on a large plate and top each one with a square of chocolate.

Preheat the grill. Thread 2 marshmallows onto each skewer and cook over hot coals for about 2 minutes, turning constantly until the marshmallows are melted and blackened. Let cool slightly.

Put the marshmallows on top of the chocolate squares and sandwich together with the remaining cookies. Gently ease out the skewers and serve the s'mores as soon as the chocolate melts.

herb, lemon, and garlic marinade

2 sprigs of rosemary

2 sprigs of thyme

4 bay leaves

2 large garlic cloves, coarsely chopped

pared zest of 1 unwaxed lemon

1 teaspoon cracked black peppercorns

1 cup extra virgin olive oil

MAKES ABOUT 1½ CUPS

Strip the rosemary and thyme leaves from the stalks and put in a mortar. Add the bay leaves, garlic, and lemon zest and pound with a pestle to release the aromas.

Put the mixture in a bowl and add the peppercorns and olive oil. Set aside to infuse until ready to use.

creamy coleslaw

8 oz. white cabbage, shredded

6 oz. carrots, grated, about 1½ cups

½ white onion, thinly sliced

1 teaspoon sea salt

2 teaspoons sugar

1 tablespoon white wine vinegar

¼ cup mayonnaise

2 tablespoons heavy cream

1 tablespoon whole-grain mustard

sea salt and freshly ground black pepper

SERVES 4

Put the cabbage, carrots, and onion in a colander and sprinkle with the salt, sugar, and vinegar. Stir well and let drain over a bowl for 30 minutes.

Squeeze out excess liquid from the vegetables and put them in a large bowl. Put the mayonnaise, cream, and mustard in a separate bowl and mix well, then stir into the cabbage mixture. Season to taste with salt and pepper and serve. Store in the refrigerator for up to 3 days.

basics

barbecue sauce

1 cup crushed tomatoes

½ cup maple syrup

2 tablespoons light molasses

2 tablespoons tomato ketchup

2 tablespoons white wine vinegar

3 tablespoons Worcestershire sauce

1 tablespoon Dijon mustard

1 teaspoon garlic powder

¼ teaspoon hot paprika

sea salt and freshly ground black pepper

MAKES ABOUT 2 CUPS

Mix all the ingredients in a small saucepan, bring to a boil, and simmer gently for 10 to 15 minutes until reduced slightly and thickened. Season to taste with salt and pepper and let cool.

Pour into an airtight container and store in the refrigerator for up to 2 weeks.

creamy corn salsa

1 ear of fresh corn, husk removed

2 red chiles, such as serrano

1 ripe tomato, diced

1 garlic clove, crushed

freshly squeezed juice of ½ lime

1 tablespoon maple syrup

2 tablespoons sour cream

sea salt and freshly ground black pepper

SERVES 6

Preheat an outdoor grill or broiler until hot. Add the corn and cook for about 15 minutes, turning frequently, until charred on all sides. Let cool.

Repeat with the chiles and broil until the skins are charred all over. Transfer to a bowl, cover with a cloth, and let cool.

Using a sharp knife, cut down all sides of the corn cob to remove the kernels and put them in a bowl. Peel and seed the chile peppers, chop the flesh, then add to the corn. Stir in all the remaining ingredients, season to taste with salt and pepper, then serve.

index

conversion charts

Weights and measures have been rounded up
or down slightly to make measuring easier.

VOLUME EQUIVALENTS:

American	Metric	Imperial
1 teaspoon	5 ml	
1 tablespoon	15 ml	
¼ cup	60 ml	2 fl. oz.
⅓ cup	75 ml	2½ fl. oz.
½ cup	125 ml	4 fl. oz.
⅔ cup	150 ml	5 fl. oz. (¼ pint)
¾ cup	175 ml	6 fl. oz.
1 cup	250 ml	8 fl. oz.

WEIGHT EQUIVALENTS: MEASUREMENTS:

Imperial	Metric	Inches	Cm
1 oz.	25 g	¼ inch	5 mm
2 oz.	50 g	½ inch	1 cm
3 oz.	75 g	¾ inch	1.5 cm
4 oz.	125 g	1 inch	2.5 cm
5 oz.	150 g	2 inches	5 cm
6 oz.	175 g	3 inches	7 cm
7 oz.	200 g	4 inches	10 cm
8 oz. (½ lb.)	250 g	5 inches	12 cm
9 oz.	275 g	6 inches	15 cm
10 oz.	300 g	7 inches	18 cm
11 oz.	325 g	8 inches	20 cm
12 oz.	375 g	9 inches	23 cm
13 oz.	400 g	10 inches	25 cm
14 oz.	425 g	11 inches	28 cm
15 oz.	475 g	12 inches	30 cm
16 oz. (1 lb.)	500 g		
2 1b.	1 kg		

OVEN TEMPERATURES:

110°C	(225°F)	Gas ¼
120°C	(250°F)	Gas ½
140°C	(275°F)	Gas 1
150°C	(300°F)	Gas 2
160°C	(325°F)	Gas 3
180°C	(350°F)	Gas 4
190°C	(375°F)	Gas 5
200°C	(400°F)	Gas 6
220°C	(425°F)	Gas 7
230°C	(450°F)	Gas 8
240°C	(475°F)	Gas 9